JEFF NUTTALL'S WAKE ON

This book is dedicated to
Sara, Daniel, Toby and Tim N
Amanda, Tom and Sam Por
Jill Richards;
and in memory of
Jane Nuttall (1927–2002)

and Jeff Nuttall (1933–2004)

Edited by Michael Horovitz
New Departures #33

Both Inside Covers: Photograph of the first Brenda's Boyfriends front line in May 1990
by George Perkin (see p32)

Jeff Nuttall's Wake on Paper
Edited by Michael Horovitz
New Departures #33

Published in 2004 by New Departures, PO Box 9819, London W11 2GQ

www.connectotel.com/PoetryOlympics
bricolage92@hotmail.com

Designed by Satpaul Bhamra with Michael Horovitz and Jamie Wilkes

This book will be best sampled alongside three other current Nuttall collections: the *Jeff Nuttall's Wake On CD* compilation (see p38 & back cover); *Jeff Nuttall: A Celebration* (available from Arc Publications, Nanholme Mill, Shaw Wood Road, Todmorden, Lancs OL14 6DA); and the monumental 262-page *Selected Poems*, one of the last jobs Jeff completed (available from Salt Publishing, POB 937, Great Wilbraham, PDO, Cambridge CB1 5JX).

All but five of the Nuttall poems in this book and on the *Jeff Nuttall's Wake On CD* selection appear in the Salt *Selected*, to which bran-tub acknowledgment is gratefully made.
The version of *Three Scenes: North of England* recorded at the London Young Vic Theatre's memorial 'Celebration of Frances Horovitz' (Track 7 of NDCD#34) was substantially revised for the 2003 Salt selection. *For Fran* was first published in New Departures #16, 1983; the poems on pp27 & 28 first appeared in New Departures #13, 1981.

Many thanks to all the friends who helped facilitate all three productions, including: Arc Publications, Robert Bank, Satpaul Bhamra, John Calder, Andy Cleyndert, Martin Davison, Valerie Doulton, Chris & Jen Emery, Adam Horovitz, Ashley Knowles, John May, Sara & Toby Nuttall, The People Show, Mandy Porter, Jill Richards, Dave Russell, Salt Publishing, The Skilbecks, John Latimer Smith, Tony Ward, Mark Wildig, Jamie Wilkes, Ann Wolff. Apologies to anyone accidentally omitted.

A CIP catalogue record for this book is available from the British Library.

ISBN 0-902689-22-3

CONTENTS

My earliest memory of Jeff dates back to a sunny evening in the mid-1960s. We knew of each other, and that we both loved jazz, but I don't think we'd met before. We strolled out of the Park Hotel, Cardiff amidst a garrulous gaggle of poets en route for the party to launch what turned out to be a notoriously shambolic Commonwealth Poets' Conference. Suddenly, Jeff scatted into a fair imitation of Armstrong's succulent opening to *Struttin' with Some Barbecue*. Instantly recognising a fellow spirit, I chimed in with the harmonies, and a friendship was born which I feel undeservedly lucky to be able to continue by producing this booklet, and its other arm *Jeff Nuttall's Wake On CD* – as well as its heart in the form of the Wake itself, on May Day 2004 at St John's Church, Waterloo.

The blurb to Jeff's *Pig* (Fulcrum Press, 1969), probably [co]written by him, states: "Jeff Nuttall was brought up on the Welsh border. He passed through art school, National Service, marriage, protest and various much publicised underground activities, experiencing all these things in the light of a vision which derives from his upbringing and is reflected in his creative writing .... [which] weaves elements of nausea and uncomfortable violence into a fabric of lyric delicacy." Spot-on.

He was a creator, comedian and prophet who saw in his teens that the gratuitous terror-bombings of Dresden, Hiroshima and Nagasaki left little hope for global survival save in the pursuit of love, art and non-military intelligence. He articulated this conviction in *Bomb Culture* (1968) and other of his forty books. He hated the hi-jacking of mid-1960s human-scale counter-culture by the soulless forces of profiteering and realpolitik.

His five adult decades were spent inspiring hundreds of students, mainly at Northern art schools, to fulfil their potentials, and in later years he played cameo roles for films, TV ... and money. But he never stopped working on his personal extra-curricular mission.

He was a pioneer of mixed-media happenings, performance art and improvised theatre, and a cornet player-singer-pianist-bandleader who regularly emulated his mentor Fats Waller in the outsize high spirits and satirical energy with which he propelled ever more multifarious formations and audiences to mutual euphoria.

However desperate the circumstances, or ghastly the opposition, Jeff hardly ever lost his puckish sense of humour, nor his instinct for bringing out the best from people of every stripe and hue. He was a Blakean good mate to "everything that lives is holy", and an exemplary engineer of amiably unfettered spontaneity – as witness his wonted instruction to motley troupes of musos often schooled in seriously variant idioms: "Play the tune, fuck about for ten minutes, then play the tune again." This may sound random, but on its day, Jeff's fucking about was of the highest order.

His landscaper's eye, improviser's ear and benignly sensous imagination enabled him to record sharp impressions even when half-drunk – as in his first poem here, and on the CD.

Return Trip traces Jeff's musings on revisiting for an afternoon, after 30 or so years away, the Orcop Valley where he'd spent his first eight years. He had retained a dream of this early childhood, which he took to be purely pantheistic, from which he derived his recurrent landscape imagery and feelings of common purpose with such artists as Samuel Palmer, Traherne and Hopkins. But when he actually got back there he discovered that these forms were fast disappearing – and that wild nature itself was the very thing masking and devouring them. He found orchards decayed, fallen stiles and wood fences broken, lanes completely overgrown, vanishing hedgerows, barns and cottages ruined or demolished. Nature was, in fact, reclaiming the landscape in which his vision was rooted, destroying the man-made continuum he had grown up with and loved.

Jeff's elliptical handling of these themes, at once imagistic and onomatopoeic, brings his beloved Dylan Thomas to mind. Jeff's quest is a less religious, more probingly intellectual one. And yet the metaphysical lifebelts with which he attempts to salvage his oceanic memories afford him no more enduring solace than Thomas's paradise regained in *Fern Hill* did him. In Jeff's haunted return the exaltation of *Fern Hill* is replaced by a mood of wry submission to the dispassionate turning of the planet.

Return Trip is a more shaken kaleidoscope of flashbacks than Thomas's, but it does revel in one unbesmirched earliest memory of all. The thrice repeated word "Golden" at the outset recalls a succession of apparently golden musical chords Jeff Nuttall heard, ancestral and epiphanous, in the multi-voiced sunshine of his pram.

William Burroughs, another of his mentors, relished the way "Jeff Nuttall *touches* his words", and Jeff made more sense than anyone I've read – including Burroughs himself – of the old magus's literary cut-up programme (just compare the version of *Three Scenes: North of England* on p19 with the one on our CD).

In 1990, Jeff summarised his approach, in most of the genres he tackled, as: "I make a line out of a rhythmic figure. The previous figure suggests the subsequent one. The rhythmic figures owe much to Charlie Parker's saxophone phrasing".

Jeff's bones are pushing up bluebells in Abergavenny now, but the lights of his vast cornucopia of golden work and play will shine bright for many moons hence. When Parker died 50 years ago, Jazzland's walls sang out "BIRD LIVES' – and so too today, wherever Mermaid Taverns stay open, let sound-systems of the post-war worlds proclaim: 'JEFF NUTTALL LIVES'.

Michael Horovitz, 25 April 2004

RETURN TRIP

Golden in this spot. The oak with its root-seats – a germinal image.
So many gone. The roots' bark cup, level cocoa-cup helping of red sand,
        acorns embedded.
All buried, the bole choked.

Golden this valley with bubbling
Vomit of centuries spilled along barrows, down
Ant-hills, spaced writing of ridges.
Clay cones, all levelled, uprooted.
    "What I loved was never nature, was culture.
    What stops pantheism's vindication is this fact:
    Lines and languages of land I long for,
    What eradicates them's rank grass, river clay."

Golden they spoke, the strata of systems. Whence now their whispers?
        Who do they talk to?
        Trees?
"Is this, like them, ghost?" the man might wonder.
He sells wrecked cars where my pram rocked (playground father's village
        school – oak limbs still heave corn-winds overhead)
Ghost, this fat drunk falling up the lane with whisky in his fist
        (can't leave it in the car)
A wraith?

"... look round? Used to live here ..."
Song, that wood-throng throat comes rising now through alcohol,
Defence against the car-man's kids
Come to laugh at the tears of a fat apparition.

Was I gone structures then, and they me hence?
Where's poetry's power when the old house stands?
Kitchen and breakfast room: "The Prime Minister has an important
        announcement."
Dining room, drawing room – "Do you remember one September
        afternoon?"
Landing and nursery, housemaid's thirsty vagina – "Ay, dunna tell yer mam."
Brown sandstone, buttressed and gabled – the same place clearly.

So is it the same time too, surrounded by change,
An island where wraiths revive?
If times are so shuffled who is the impotent ghost
When interleaved with a living man's potency? What
Potency ever, with No-Time certainly housing identity?
How does the nursery, unchanged, stand
Gainst drifts of rain, red clay, new grass – tender, persistent, indifferent?

She clings to my fragments (several men saw them, sun
severe on her velveteen, light hard on his
helmet hair, clutched amongst clovers in
that meadow where the straight track ran)
– She gives her vagina; he palms some certainty.
"Self," says hardening blood, says calmly.
"Where?" the heartsblood, fading, dyingly denies.
"Where were we then?"
The question's set against the other
Current question: "Who, now, are we?
Does it ever matter?"
Or matter who we will be, love, and one another,
Under shuffled truths, the grass, rain, red clay,
Tender and indifferent?

Scissor. Trunk. Elephants.
Razor. Lace. Monkeys.

Scissor the elephant's trunk.
Razor monkeys lace the elements in rhubarb bushes.

Hush said the
weasel who now
could do nothing
but squeak.

THE NURSERY CUPBOARD IS LOUD WITH THE BRAYS
OF THE BUGLE-EYED NANNY GOATS.

Slash the pumpernicle beach balls. *Bounce*
The star-spun rubber meat on a pandy-bat prong.

Child's raw squall. The indigestion of the gouty teddy-bear
A mother with icy fingers
Is scratching weasel-squeaks across the window glass.

BRADFORD SATURDAY MORNING BUS

God will do to be thanked for the gut-searching lurch of the bus;
Arc to arc curve of the camber to twist of intestine,
Space recognised by acids exploring the bend in the piping
– God will serve for a passing ovation.

HALIFAX RAILWAY

Bestowed the teeth on an ambitious jaw,
Bestowed ambitious jaws on an ingenious skull,
Bestowed an army of Tykes (twenty pints a day)
Brawling under the company banner – Lancashire and Yorkshire –
The scopping jaws in action – ten-hour day.

Spat the carbone and sulphur into night fires,
Massed the moorland dark around the coalgas lanterns all along the vale,
Blew a keen blade of male invention through the blasphemy of Wesley's
        treadmills,
Surely laughed like an unthrottled furnace
When Queen Victoria offered up her thanks.

SUICIDE NOTE

Float me into no-more. Feathernest me into home again.
Raise me when I'm blown for –
To and fro in the roaming rain.
Join me with the known core.
No blame. I'm strong and sown and sane.

DIARY ENTRY

London. It is '68, the year after the year of love. The revolution is still rumbling on the streets of Paris. The art schools and the universities are still occupied. The whole thing was precipitated in this country by poets and poetry. The Albert Hall reading saw the butterfly of hippiedom emerge from the chrysalis of CND. The centres were still bookshops and poetry readings were still as important as rock concerts on the revolutionary cultural calendar. Mike Horovitz is running a reading in the bar of a London theatre. He is helped in this by a young and pleasant woman who is responsible for bar events.

Pete Brown has been drumming. The poems have come fast and furious – Ivor Cutler, Spike Hawkins, Mike, me, with a tidal wave of applause following each.

I am on a roll of success. *Bomb Culture* has just come out to widespread rave reviews. My poems are in Penguin and I've escaped secondary modern schoolteaching to a job at Bradford Art School.

I stagger off the stand, breaking through the applause like a swimmer, grab a bottle of Newcastle Brown, pour it, drink it and turn as the house-manager passes.

'Kiss me,' I say.
'No,' she says.

MH & JN at Polymaths, Centrepoint House, '93

THE PEOPLE SHOW

Jeff co-founded The People Show, an innovatory theatre troupe, with Mark Long in 1967. He travelled with, wrote for and acted in it for five years, and continued providing input on and off over the subsequent decades. The photograph above documents a moment from Show #92, *Whistlestop*, at London's Bush Theatre in 1987: l to r, Charlie Dore, Mark Long, George Khan (tenor sax), and Jeff (cornet) as Boyle Hannigan, an Irish gambler, murderer, doctor, musician-singer and demon lover – an All-Round Bad Sort.

Christine Entwisle, who is directing the current Show, wrote the following farewell to Jeff for this book on 24 April 2004: "*I am rushing this off in my lunch break. I am very anxious. This is because I am working with The People Show. Again. I swore I wouldn't after last time. But it gets you that way. It makes people anxious. The people in it. The people who watch it. And although we are many years on from when you kicked it off, and none of the original members are in this show, it still reminds me of you. It is wonderful. It is funny. It is fat. You gave me a shiny Beauty and the Beast 'Good Luck' card a few years ago when I was working at Theatre Clwyd. I have spent the last three months looking for it. I can't find it. Anyway, I've got other stuff. Better stuff. The recording of the radio show we did. And the very clear memory of your eyes twinkling in the tea breaks. Warm with anarchy.*"

Excerpts from an interview Jeff Nuttall gave to John May in London's Chelsea Arts Club, in December 1984. Some of this transcript can be heard on JEFF NUTTALL'S WAKE ON CD, which in turn includes material not transcribed below.

JM: What were the circumstances that led you to write 'Bomb Culture'?
JN: I'd had a couple of preliminary stabs at it and then I went on holiday to Wales and suddenly it all fell into place: the three strains – the pop strain, the protest strain and the art strain – and the merging of them in some kind of movement that felt that every one of these three strains had something to offer in the state of emergency. Which was the failure of CND, because it became clear in the early 1960s that massive crowds and massive civil disobedience were ineffectual and nobody in Parliament was bothered about them one iota.

Several people came up with the idea of cultural warfare, of seeding pacifist and subversive elements in the popular culture. The popular culture having been almost purely a commercial enterprise previously (if you can say purely commercial), art not being concerned with being popular at all, and protest eschewing art as though art were self-indulgent and were not sufficiently puritan, not sufficiently ethically motivated.

Just for a while they merged and that was what *Bomb Culture* was about, and I happened to be around while it was merging. I wrote it in 1967, which was the year of mounting protest against the Vietnam War, and 1968 was the student upheaval. In Paris, as everybody knew at the time – though people have kind of forgotten – they did open prisons and burn the stock exchange and it really did look as though this was it, this was spontaneous revolution.

I was very much concerned about the Bomb, and about sowing this element of dissent into the popular culture, that would ultimately lead to inevitable disarmament and probably the dissolution of nations, and the setting up of a common human consciousness. We all believed it then you know! It looked as though it was bloody near inevitable, because the change in thinking and the change in the culture between '65 and '67 was amazing.

Hunter S. Thompson talks very eloquently about how it all seemed *completely* inevitable, the victory was there, it was just a question of letting it happen. So my writing *Bomb Culture* was a signing off from it really, a kind of retraction to going back to writing poetry which was concerned with poetry and concerned with the interpretation of a highly personal vision, and making art which owed nothing to anybody and didn't have to contain any kind of message at all.

You talk in 'Bomb Culture' about the gap that's opened up between generations in the atomic age.

The gap is between those people who have experienced a notion of the world as a continuum and those people who have not had that experience. I don't want to be patronising or come on like an uncle, but I think I can remember up until 1945 believing that one way or another there might be some awful things that would happen, but the world would continue. That whatever went wrong, in the fullness of time, it would eventually come right. You can't remember that. You might wish to remember it. You might be able to imagine it. But I can remember when *every*body believed it. I think this has done something quite disastrous to social ethics.

Is the Bomb shaping artistic consciousness all over the world?

What one wants from a Bomb-conscious artist is an antithesis to the Bomb. One wants opposition to the Bomb, and one can't have opposition to the Bomb which in itself has its roots in the existence of the Bomb. What one actually wants from one's artists is gestures and statements and experiences that are going to perpetually put before humanity, before the public, before society, a way of thinking which is not part of the internal, competitive, war-power system.

.... You have to overcome the difficulty of loving your state, your condition. Anybody can look at a sunset and say goo goo goo, how nice, or cuddle a baby, or fall in love with a pretty girl or a pretty boy. That's the easy bit. The difficult bit is somehow loving a state which includes the obscene and the vicious and the dreadful and the painful and loving *that*. *Really* loving it, not tolerating it or blessing it or forgiving it or putting up with it or grinning and bearing it, but *really loving it* as being an integral and unavoidable part of the kind of creature you are and the state of existence you inhabit.

That's where I stand at the moment. Far too much, somewhere hovering behind the existence of the Bomb, is the notion that ... it's not worth saving. It's so disgusting, it's so foul, so corrupt, it's so *old* and so *boring* and it's so *diseased* that you might as well ....

– *Just wipe it clean* –

.... Yes; and what you've got to really do is create some kind of cultural movement which would be against that. How it's to happen now I really don't know. I don't feel despairing because I think that – I'm 52 now – I really didn't expect to see the age of 30.

THREE SCENES: LONDON

(Euston Road at Lunchtime. Pub in Bloomsbury. Intercity – Euston to Manchester. All on the eve of the second Thatcherite election victory.)

Grinds her muscular ecology and the outbroke light
Is a gaudy plastic Chinese chippy dragon's
Roaring I could measure up to while the lunchtime crowdstrut promises are
 realised.
Drag back these wanderers. Hymn them. She's going to get in again.

Her lipswelling signs are suspect. One fuck spells glutted landscapes.

NOT ON NOT ON squeak the windowgnomes
NOWHERE NEAR whisper the young in their conventional, squalorchic
 trenches.
Some way to make a dirty-haired mere rope of a girl
Feel her crumpled red corduroy twopiece to have been besmirched,
Wild wind adrift to make relevancy easy.

Chiselled teak cheeks.
Sensuality of his innocuous lips
Forms a proposition, provokes a dedicated purpose
To flood the lot with sudden, stinking stop of sperm.

If Thatcher knew how to usurp the realm of floating imagery, Blair recognised that the route to success lay in the continuation of the monetarism Thatcher had established, and that his means to this success would have to be the fluidity of verbal definition that has sprung up through Structuralist jargon and computer-speak. If you can file and call it 'storing to memory', if you can transfer and call it 'downloading', if you can call the Dionysian 'abject', and revolution 'reconstruction', if you can call a slump a 'recession', then you can call consumer capitalism 'Labour'. Before this you must step into the Labour leadership at a time of crisis; then you must rely on the tacit hope of Labour voters that your piece-by-piece abandonment of Socialism is an electioneering strategy to be mercifully rectified after the election. Finally you must convince the disillusioned new Tories, Dome-bred and nourished on fashion, image and 'attitude', that Labour, a mere word, is banner enough under which to continue the Thatcherite principles of brute careerism and greed.

'Attitude' comes, beneath the Dome, to mean animation, rhetoric, hyperbole, hubris and gaga optimism, and is, of course, as empty as Blair's smile which is proving, as catastrophes accumulate on Indian frontiers, in French provincial town squares, in hospitals, schools and prisons, as irremovable as that of the late Reginald Bosanquet.

But emptiness is the Post-Modern mode. The void, rectangular spaces of the Saatchi Gallery, the slack, unlined, unpatterned and untextured fabric of the perpetually casual dress-style, the vapid nursery humour of successful sitcoms, the gap-headed infantilism of football fanatics, acid-house ravers, the rigid and dedicated refusal of all thought, passion, love, wit or honour is the first necessary element in the style of our time and Blair has found out how to embody it.

Thus, like Thatcher he will remain in power far longer than we can afford him, wreaking havoc merrily in all our quarters until we must face reality because fact will be all there is left to face, the fact of the blood on our own hands in Kosovo, the fact of Milosevic's victims dispersed permanently beyond their own frontiers, the fact of the Chinese nuclear arsenal, for fabrications will run dry under the Rock and Roll Dome and there is a great big nothing at all in the Millennium Dome to revive them.

– from 'Art and the Degradation of Awareness', Calder Publications 2001

The Nuttalls outside the back of their house in Wyke in 1970 – Jane, Toby, Sarah, Jeff, Tim and Daniel

Jeff and Jill at home in Abergavenny, 1995

Frances Horovitz (1938–1983) in the Cotswolds, 1973

FOR FRAN

Never more than a meadow's whisp separate from the wind.
Head of flute-bone, moor-bone, sea-bone
Cut to an oblique grace.

Never far from a temple peal
Lifting the skin at a high blithe eye.
Flesh thrilled that never knew blood.

A schoolmarm, arch as a rose-bower,
Proud as a spring nipple.
Declension of her inclination, gender of her cloven kind.

Get out, heat. Get out of my cooling.
Out, itch. Out of my peace.
Fester in fears. Mouth illiteracies.
Crawl back to the mediocrities.

The ivory graces its smiling insidious tunnel
Trapped in yak bells.

THREE SCENES: NORTH OF ENGLAND

(Haworth Moor in Autumn – late afternoon. The Nuclear Early Warning spheres on the North Yorkshire Moors. The beach at Robin Hood's Bay with much-repaired stone and concrete ramp.)

Vault, a vault of burned herbs, stove of toast.
Horizon into which the SOS bulbs are studded.
Rose spilled thinly, prodigiously: great wheel concrete dollop.
Turdcobble galaxy and button-mushrooms humming down the universal
　　curtain.

Generous was its supply in deference to the diluted density of colour; rose;
Last wan dip of a day's eyelid.
Spread, enfolding granite custard of the Robin Hood's Bay slipway,
Whence my wild son sews his seam of ponytracks.
Gone out of sight, the rose of it, let into, over and out, out.

Spilled and reflected. Water (no thicker than).
Flat flood of petalwash.
To, back. There and fro in seatrance.
Daygleam petal stung still, delicately poisonous.

Spacewound, Haworth to Hebden,
Burnishing its pain.
Vertical grassgold, jet shade,
Pussywillow clouds and heather crochetwork.

MARGARET THATCHER AND THE FOX

On snub toe socketed in speckled magenta
The predator sneak-dances.
Or is it his muzzle that nuzzles the poison-spot pit
Breathing a purple wine pressed out of
Goose-gorse, worm-wood, fern-frond?

Dusk on the mushroom, on Aaron-sprig essence that
Festered for our turning arses – Pandy 1954.

She got in. England rots in terror of the mainland.
She hoists a flag. She wags and is a battleaxe –
All it takes.

England's secret surviving mind
Talks smart in fox-yelps,
In the prick-sprout over leaf-mould
Flickerlit through fern.
The tart mind of England is a sparkling schizophrenic
Private in unique clusters of celandine-impulse,
Is Viking, Norman, Celt, Iberian, Jew, Anglo-Saxon,
Dances dogtooth and strapwork cultures down fox-runs of puce bugles.

Humped cherrywool and a cockatoo whisp.
He drives into the armpit – old suede, fresh sweat.
Her face erupts in its concerned blood.

Yelp of a hurt dog / squall of a toothless throat –
Echo of klaxon of cock-crowing source.
She stirs uneasily, fingers her gin. Tits sting.

His whole bulk sighs, then trembles to its tips.
Eyes so opened wide to all new spectacle transparency surpasses raindrops,
        dewponds, spangled spiderwebs. In profile
Iris waterlight holds sky.

Bundled in a plastic bestiary
Ingestion pops the sudden gratitude of pools for first rain.
Her bruised face is pestered. Giggles tug and pass. Imminent kiss sucks.

Your sleepy musk is a season's tang. Incline your sad head like a winter
afternoon.
No drink but milk for that quick naked lip.
The afternoon is milk.

Your husk in sleep grunts sighs and moaned affections
Betrays the tiny animal inside
Soft pelt at shut fork breathing breathing ...
Who puts saucers full of milk for baby hedgehogs these days anyway?

FOR MY SON

Mind how you go. Don't
Snap your drinking eyes so hard
You bruise the day. Don't spur the day
                    to blind you.

Mind how you go. Don't
Magnify the day's electric impulse
Till your eldritch pleasure fells the halfchick sky
                    to crush you.

Mind how you go. Don't
Flush such blood up to your face's measure.
Pleasure's numbed in pressures
Drumming at the shut pores
                    that secrete you.

Please don't
Glut your sore-pink self to show
Your flesh past dimmer glow
To edgy glister; don't let
Juices wet you like a blister running –
Like a sticky bud let lose you. Know
                    the knives are out,

The blades are keen in miracle.
Your high bright sickle sheen
Could cut to stumps the You I've sown.
                    Mind how you go.

MEDIEVAL: ENGLAND

Tree fools
Bell Cap Leaves
Nodding jongleurs
(the hiss of rustling
leaf green underbellies
distant bells from the old green wedding)
Catatonic saraband
With a dip and a hiss
With a grave absurdity of courtiers ...

The ass's ears of milky ash ...

The lime is a pennant
For the sad mock tournament
Sometimes a funeral
Where nothing really dies but the rapture
The sighs of the wind applauding
An old green ritual. Pennants and puns
Mocking the empty stand
Where the bridegroom/knight/jester
Stood before leaving to leap summer woods
– mad in his antlers.

MOTHER AND DAUGHTER

They talk. I imagine shy men, habitual voyeurs who stood on the stone step,
wanker's hands clutching a rained-on trilby.

Where did they sit and how did they lie? Like me, on the edge of the
        Put-U-Up,
a little bit over-defiant, like me in the public park,
more than a little bit pissed?

And did they notice the nudges and sidelong looks,
the mutual pampering mutual smoothing of midnight charms,
sense the unspoken campaigns planned?

Did they wake to a blank wall just before dawn
and an empty nest left warm in the sheets, to hear the purring,
the sleek black blandishments out on the cold stair?

Did they creep to the door
to hear the holiest secrets discussed as an old joke,
then open the door, to see a pair of black pedigree cats
rub side to voluptuous side as they picked through the quills of a dead falcon?

And the bee on wheels has laments on a stick
Wags weepy banners with gypsy ribbons

And the distant elephants splendid over the gherkin moors
Wave sad trunks in acknowledgement of such a well-deported grief.

Lachrymose the glove trees close. The knitted pink of a tadpole harness
Is plain as a pearl beneath their gossiping midnight cross-stitch.

The tiny wheeled bee has the sky on a stick
Idly waves as she buzzes through the afternoon
Kicking the tears around like bean-tins.

The surly postman with a pocketful of cold pudding
 shall bear her beasts,
Wild antelopes and boss-eyed bears antic on the back
 lawn of "Oakdene".
Spifflicate water-buffalo drunk on rainbow fish will
 snore beside the oval father where he basks.
A tropic tiger-sun on Sundays paints the GPO menagerie,
 a zebra grill of liquorice and marmalade.

And rising from the lilac dew of her gracious Sabbath alcohol
She will walk abroad amongst the franked panthers and the
 first-class cougars.
A gentle hand will change the rhinos into bumble-birds.
Fond horned horses nuzzlemusk the mossy liquids
Of her most exclusive byres.

Every night is a curtain over deeper dark
(Somebody calls from the far shore of the moon lake).

Every tock of the bedside clock
Is the ticket on a silence stretched out of measurement
(No truth to the music that's not beyond reach
Mountains of midnight away).

Claw though the curtains
Penis or reaching hand
Extended for anyone's touch –
Out through the levels of threat and malevolence,
Breathing rough discords of need
For the pearl-studded oysterpalm,
Sky at your knackers' back,
Angel-smile frisking blue butterfly,
Siren defined out of touch
Into vaults of beyond so dark they can only be lost.

2001

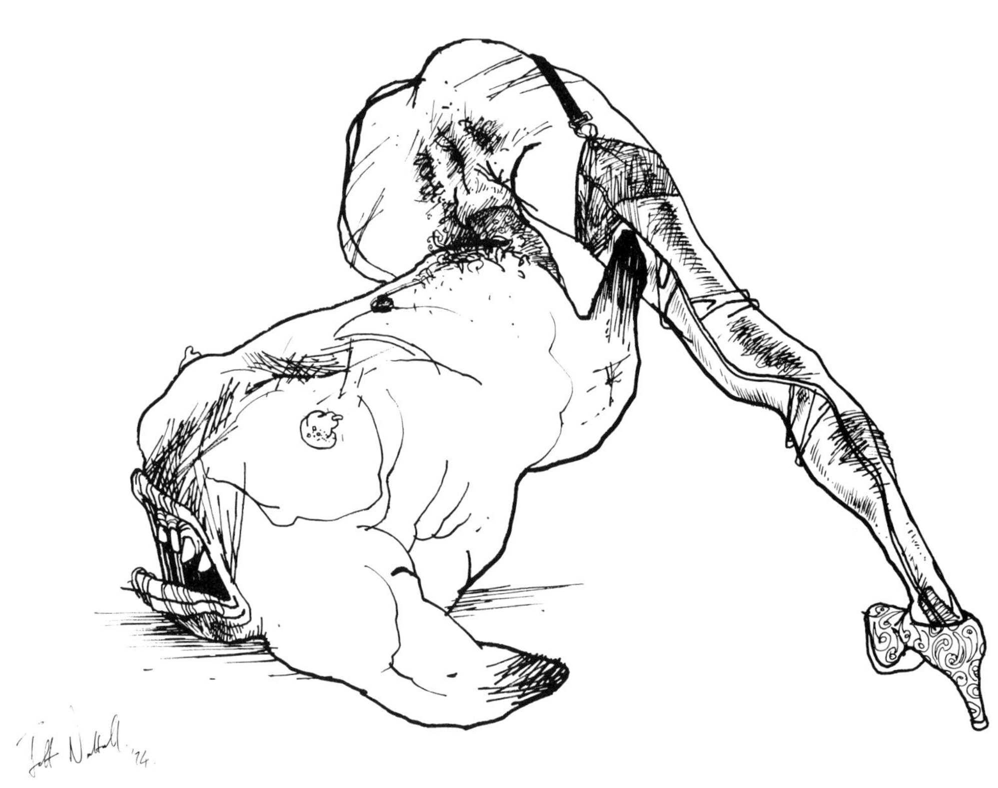

... At orgasm I'm home.
The snapped elastic full pulled,
Climactic visions,
Spastic's kickjoint, bloodwilled,
Thrilled discord at control's collapse,
Sour resolution of a sinister perhaps,
Disprove proof ...

(middle stanza of 'Windows'
– see page 3 of Selected Poems,
Salt Publishing)

One of Jeff's illustrations for Michael Horovitz's epic, *The Woverhampton Wanderer*, 1971

Jeff's late 1980s drawing of the Buttershaw's (who can be heard on Tracks 10 & 11 of JEFF NUTTALL'S WAKE ON CD – see back cover): Jeff on cornet, Warren Latham (tenor sax), Chris Howse (banjo) and Helen Minshall (tuba).

Top Left: Jeff's poster for Brenda's Boyfriends, who provide Tracks 4 & 6 of the CD. Martin Davison, who now leads the band, remembers:
"He produced this in no time at all from two photographs with the aid of photocopier, black felt pen & Tippex. A striking image still in use."
The Boyfriends' first front line of (l to r) Martin Davison, Eddie Falkiner, Jeff and Liam de Staic, was snapped in May 1990 on the shot that adorns both of this book's inside covers. It was named by Jeff after Brenda McDermott, who was landlady of The Edinburgh Castle in Barnes, where the band played until the pub closed down in February 1996. The latest incarnation of the Boyfriends plays every Wednesday at The Halfway House in Priest's Bridge, also in Barnes.

– from New Departures #13. In 1981 I asked Jeff to design a poster for our 'World's Best Jam' gig at the Wyvern Theatre, Swindon. He came up with the above, depicting, l to r: myself, Lol Coxhill, Adrian Mitchell, John Cooper Clarke, Roy Fisher on piano, and himself as piglet.

The ones he "couldn't do" were, l to r: Stan Tracey, Pete Brown, Christopher Logue and Fran Landesman.

On JEFF NUTTALL'S WAKE ON CD, you can hear: Lol and myself on Track 1; Pete Brown and myself on Tracks 1 & 15; and of course, Jeff himself on all 16 tracks. [MH]

Jeff's drawing for Monologue One

MONOLOGUE ONE

I am happy to be wearing all my clothes.

I usually do these days. This is not to say that I do not remove my clothes when I wash my body. I do. On almost every occasion when I wash my body I remove my clothes. All of them.

And on almost every occasion when I intend sleep I remove most of them. Sometimes I remove all of them but usually, when I approach my bed wholly unclothed, it is not with the intention of sleep. Not immediate sleep anyway.

When I remove my clothes the first garment I remove is my tie. This, of course, is on the occasions when I am wearing a tie. The second garment is my jacket unless the jacket has been already removed or has not, on that occasion, ever been worn.

The shoes follow and then my trousers. I am secretly rather proud of the way in which I remove my trousers. I unbuckle my belt, I unlatch the top, I unzip my zip and then I slide them down over my buttocks.

Having done this I balance on one foot and, with a decisive movement of my first and second fingers, I extract one foot from sock and trousers simultaneously. Changing my weight to my now naked foot I repeat this action on the other side.

I am curiously proud of the economy of motion involved but I am not going to demonstrate it now. My pride is not so great.

Lastly of course I remove my underwear which, on almost every occasion, is a garment belonging to me, designed to be worn by a male adult.

On the occasions when I take rest I do not remove all my garments.

My underwear continues to cover my torso and my loins, clinging lightly to my flesh and not wholly malodorous.

But today I am happy to be wearing all my clothes, happy also to be able to assure you that I will remain fully clothed while I am in your company.

I shall shortly leave your company.

AFTERWORD

Jeff Nuttall has gone. Remember him in cherry-stones – poet, painter, teacher, actor, musician, journalist, biographer and, in his day, fearless activist. The big man with the throwaway laugh and the deeply-held opinions. The intellectual buffoon whose charismatic presence always lifted our group beyond the ordinary and sometimes threw it into confusion.

He was not an abstemious man and was well aware of the risks he took. He spoke of death in terms of its untidiness and irony; he died listening to jazz with a glass of wine in his hand. He was a well-known man; to some he was *Bomb Culture*, to others Friar Tuck, to some a critic, to others a clown. We Scriveners* knew him as a witty, often kind and occasionally bloody-minded colleague, fellow-writer and friend. We shall miss him.

Jeff was a past master at taking things out of context, with results that were sometimes exasperating and often hilarious. I wish I had the chance to show him two lines that had been arbitrarily extracted from his *oeuvre* and posted on a website dedicated to the Alexander Technique. Alas, now all I can do is hope he has found an echo of them somewhere:

Then hold my hand a bit,
I'll give you gold where we are going now.

Ann Drysdale

* Scriveners is a group of writers meeting regulary in Abergavenny, to give each other honest and informed criticism of work in progress. Jeff was instrumental in setting it up, and acted as Chair for several years. At the time of his death he was its honorary President. Ann initially wrote this appreciation for the group's journal, The Scrivener.

"… as long as 'global politics' fester in lies and pea-brained Hollywooden mega-violence, it is bollocks to them and long live Jeff Nuttall."
Michael Horovitz, The Guardian, 12 January 2004

In scribbled light crawling through sharded trees
long live Jeff Nuttall
In salty jokes dropped like olive branches from a crow's beak
long live Jeff Nuttall
In the creep and pounce of progress, biting under the fur of the future
long live Jeff Nuttall
In the distilled image, the refracted word
long live Jeff Nuttall
In the arms of the triple-whisky goddess
long live Jeff Nuttall
Nestled in the shadowy bosom of Blorenge
long live Jeff Nuttall

Adam Horovitz

Photograph of Blorenge taken from Jeff's graveside at his funeral on 12 January 2004 by AH. It was Jeff's favourite mountain

PUBLICATIONS, CDS & CASSETTES AVAILABLE FROM NEW DEPARTURES

For more information about these titles and related publications/events, visit: *www.connectotel.com/PoetryOlympics* or write (enclosing an sae if not placing an order) or email **bricolage92@hotmail.com**

Grandchildren of Albion Live on Cassette Volume One
____ (95 minutes) £8 each plus £1.50 p&p (incl VAT)* *NDC 23, ISBN 0-902689-15-0*

Grandchildren of Albion Live on CD Volume One
____ (78 minutes) £10.50 each plus £2 p&p (incl VAT)* *NDCD 24, ISBN 0-902689-16-9*
(Ifigenija Simonovic's and Adam Horovitz's sets & Donal Carroll's 2nd/3rd poems omitted)

Grandchildren of Albion Anthology
____ (400-page illustrated) £9.99 plus £3 p&p* *ND17-20, ISBN 0-902689-14-2*
(only sent for orders enclosing pre-payment in full, as very few copies remain)

Midsummer Morning Jog Log – 700-line rural rhapsody by Michael Horovitz
____ (Paperback edition) illustrated by Peter Blake, £3.50 plus £1 p&p* *ISBN 0-9504606-8-0*

Wordsounds & Sightlines: New & Selected Poems by Michael Horovitz
____ (160-page, cover by David Hockney) £6.99 plus £1 p&p* *ND31, ISBN 0-902689-20-7*

The POW! Anthology, edited by Michael Horovitz and Inge Elsa Laird
____ (108-page illustrated) £6.99 plus £1.50 p&p* *ND21–22, ISBN 0-902689-17-7*

The POP! Anthology, edited by Michael Horovitz and Inge Elsa Laird
____ (128-page illustrated) £7.99 plus £1.50 p&p* *ND25–26, ISBN 0-902689-19-3*

The POM! Anthology, edited by Michael Horovitz
____ (80-page illustrated) £5.99 plus £1 p&p* *ND32, ISBN 0-902689-21-5*

Jeff Nuttall's Wake on Paper, edited by Michael Horovitz
____ (40-page illustrated) £5 plus £1 p&p* *ND33, ISBN 0-902689-22-3*

Jeff Nuttall's Wake on CD, edited by Michael Horovitz
____ £10 plus £2 p&p* *NDCD34, ISBN 0-902689-23-1*

Please **photocopy** this form, complete with no. of copies required on left – and send to:
New Departures, PO Box 9819, London W11 2GQ, United Kingdom.
Allow 21 days for delivery (longer for outside the UK).
***If ordering outside the UK, please double the amount for postage/packing.**

I enclose a crossed cheque/postal order for £ ________ made payable to ***New Departures*** as total cost of this order including postage and packing.

Name ____________________

Address ____________________

____

Postcode ____________________